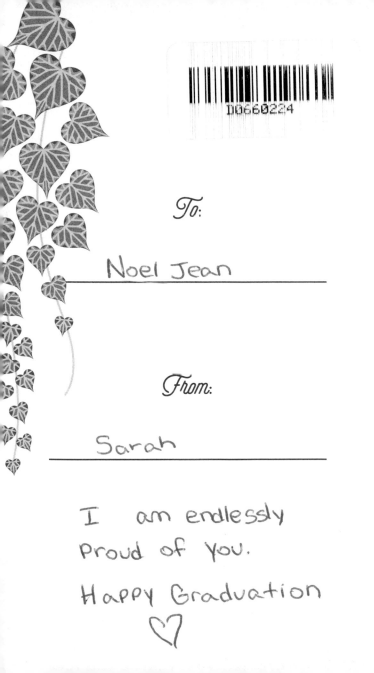

To:

Noel Jean

From:

Sarah

I am endlessly
proud of you.

Happy Graduation

Poems
on
Friendship

Poems on Friendship

STERLING
New York

STERLING
New York

An Imprint of Sterling Publishing Co., Inc.

STERLING and the distinctive Sterling logo are registered trademarks
of Sterling Publishing Co., Inc.

Compilation © 2022 Sterling Publishing Co., Inc.

ISBN 978-1-4549-4479-9

Library of Congress Control Number: 2021950892

Distributed in Canada by Sterling Publishing Co., Inc.
c/o Canadian Manda Group, 664 Annette Street
Toronto, Ontario M6S 2C8, Canada
Distributed in the United Kingdom by GMC Distribution Services
Castle Place, 166 High Street, Lewes, East Sussex BN7 1XU, England
Distributed in Australia by NewSouth Books
University of New South Wales, Sydney, NSW 2052, Australia

For information about custom editions, special sales, and premium and
corporate purchases, please contact Sterling Special Sales at
specialsales@sterlingpublishing.com.

Manufactured in the United States

2 4 6 8 10 9 7 5 3 1

sterlingpublishing.com

Interior design by Rich Hazelton

Contents

Past Friends

Good Friends

No Man Is an Island

John Donne

No man is an island,
Entire of itself,
Every man is a piece of the continent
As part of the main.
If a clod be washed away by the sea,
Europe is the less.
As well as if a promontory were.
As well as if a manor of thy friend's
Or of thine own were;
Any man's death diminishes me,
Because I am involved in mankind,
And therefore never send to know for whom the bell tolls;
It tolls for thee.

Meat Without Mirth

Robert Herrick

Eaten I have; and though I had good cheer,
I did not sup, because no friends were there.
Where mirth and friends are absent when we dine
Or sup, there wants the incense and the wine.

Inviting a Friend to Supper

Ben Jonson

To-night, grave sir, both my poor house and I
Do equally desire your company;
Not that we think us worthy such a guest,
But that your worth will dignify our feast
With those that come; whose grace may make that seem
Something, which else could hope for no esteem.
It is the fair acceptance, sir, creates
The entertainment perfect, not the cates.
Yet shall you have, to rectify your palate,
An olive, capers, or some better salad
Ushering the mutton; with a short-legged hen,
If we can get her, full of eggs, and then
Lemons, and wine for sauce: to these a coney
Is not to be despaired of for our money;
And though fowl now be scarce, yet there are clerks,
The sky not falling, think we may have larks.
I'll tell you of more, and lie, so you will come:
Of partridge, pheasant, woodcock, of which some
May yet be there; and godwit if we can;
Knat, rail, and ruff, too. Howsoe'er, my man
Shall read a piece of Virgil, Tacitus,
Livy, or of some better book to us,
Of which we'll speak our minds, amidst our meat;
And I'll profess no verses to repeat.
To this, if ought appear, which I not know of,
That will the pastry, not my paper, show of.

Digestive cheese and fruit there sure will be;
But that which most doth take my Muse and me,
Is a pure cup of rich Canary wine,
Which is the Mermaid's now, but shall be mine;
Of which had Horace, or Anacreon tasted,
Their lives, as so their lines, till now had lasted.
Tobacco, nectar, or the Thespian spring,
Are all but Luther's beer, to this I sing.
Of this we will sup free, but moderately,
And we will have no Pooly, or Parrot by;
Nor shall our cups make any guilty men
But, at our parting, we will be as when
We innocently met. No simple word
That shall be uttered at our mirthful board,
Shall make us sad next morning or affright
The liberty that we'll enjoy to-night.

Sonnet XXX

William Shakespeare

When to the sessions of sweet silent thought
I summon up remembrance of things past,
I sigh the lack of many a thing I sought,
And with old woes new wail my dear times' waste:
Then can I draw an eye, unus'd to flow,
For precious friends hid in death's dateless night,
And wreep afresh love's long since cancell'd woe,
And moan the expense of many a vanished sight:
Then can I grieve at grievances foregone,
And heavily from woe to woe tell o'er
The sad account of fore-bemoaned moan,
Which I new pay as if not paid before.
  But if the while I think on thee, dear friend,
  All losses are restor'd, and sorrows end.

Early Friendship

Aubrey de Vere

The half-seen memories of childish days,
When pains and pleasures lightly came and went;
The sympathies of boyhood rashly spent
In fearful wanderings through forbidden ways;
The vague but manly wish to tread the maze
Of life to noble ends—whereon intent,
Asking to know for what man here is sent,
The bravest heart must often pause, and gaze;
The firm resolve to seek the chosen end
Of manhood's judgment, cautious and mature—
Each of these viewless bonds binds friend to friend
With strength no selfish purpose can secure;
My happy lot is this, that all attend
That friendship which first came, and which shall
    last endure.

A Wayfaring Song

Henry van Dyke

O who will walk a mile with me
    Along life's merry way?
A comrade blithe and full of glee
Who dares to laugh out loud and free,
And let his frolic fancy play,
Like a happy child, through the flowers gay
That fill the field and fringe the way
    Where he walks a mile with me.

And who will walk a mile with me
    Along life's weary way?
A friend whose heart has eyes to see
The stars shine out o'er the darkening lea,
And the quiet rest at the end o' the day—
A friend who knows, and dares to say,
The brave, sweet words that cheer the way
    Where he walks a mile with me.

With such a comrade, such a friend,
I fain would walk till journeys end,
Through summer sunshine, winter rain,
And then?—Farewell, we shall meet again!

The Arrow and the Song

Henry Wadsworth Longfellow

I shot an arrow into the air,
It fell to earth, I knew not where;
For, so swiftly it flew, the sight
Could not follow it in its flight.

I breathed a song into the air,
It fell to earth, I knew not where;
For who has sight so keen and strong,
That it can follow the flight of song?

Long, long afterward, in an oak
I found the arrow, still unbroke;
And the song, from beginning to end,
I found again in the heart of a friend.

To My Friend

❧

Francis Thompson

When from the blossoms of the noiseful day,
Unto the hive of sleep and hushèd gloom,
Throng the dim-wingèd dreams, what dreams are they
That with the wildest honey hover home?
Oh, they that have, from many thousand thoughts
Stolen the strange sweet of ever blossomy you—
A thousand fancies in fair-coloured knots
Which you are inexhausted meadow to.
Ah, what sharp heathery honey, quick with pain
Do they bring home! It holds the night awake
To hear their lovely murmur in my brain,
And Sleeps wings have a trouble for your sake.
     Day and you dawn together: for, at the end,
     With the first light breaks the first thought—
          "My Friend!"

Friends Indeed

F. S. Barnard

Blessings on those whose faces cheer,
　　Whose hearts are always gay,
Whose words are loving and sincere,
　　Whose youth knows not decay;
Whatever be their creed,
These are my friends indeed.

Blessings on them for they can give
　　A strength to fainting hearts,
A tonic that shall make them live,
　　And still pain's sudden darts;
Whatever be their creed,
These are my friends indeed.

Blessings on them for they can lend
　　A smile to all they meet.
It matters not if stranger, friend,
　　The smile is welcome, sweet;
Whatever be their creed.
These are my friends indeed.

Emblems of Friendship

John Imrie

Friendship is a GOLDEN BAND
    Linking life with life
Heart to Heart, and hand to hand,
    Antidote to strife.

Friendship is a SILKEN CORD
    Beautiful and strong
Guarding, by each kindly word,
    Loving hearts from wrong.

Friendship is a BEACON LIGHT
    On life's rocky shore,
Brightest in our darkest night
    When the breakers roar.

Friendship is an IRON SHIELD
    Where life's cruel darts
Ever may be forced to yield
    Ere they wound true hearts.

Friendship is the GIFT OF GOD
    Freely to us given,
As the flowers that gem the sod,
    Or the light of heaven!

Travelling

William Wordsworth

This is the spot:—how mildly does the sun
Shine in between the fading leaves! the air
In the habitual silence of this wood
Is more than silent: and this bed of heath—
Where shall we find so sweet a resting-place?
Come, let me see thee sink into a dream
Of quiet thoughts, protracted till thine eye
Be calm as water when the winds are gone
And no one can tell whither. My sweet Friend,
We two have had such happy hours together
That my heart melts in me to think of it.

This Lime-tree Bower My Prison

Samuel Taylor Coleridge

Well, they are gone, and here must I remain,
This lime-tree bower my prison! I have lost
Beauties and feelings, such as would have been
Most sweet to my remembrance even when age
Had dimm'd mine eyes to blindness! They, meanwhile,
Friends, whom I never more may meet again,
On springy heath, along the hill-top edge,
Wander in gladness, and wind down, perchance,
To that still roaring dell, of which I told;
The roaring dell, o'erwooded, narrow, deep,
And only speckled by the mid-day sun;
Where its slim trunk the ash from rock to rock
Flings arching like a bridge;—that branchless ash,
Unsunn'd and damp, whose few poor yellow leaves
Ne'er tremble in the gale, yet tremble still,
Fann'd by the water-fall! and there my friends
Behold the dark green file of long lank weeds,
That all at once (a most fantastic sight!)
Still nod and drip beneath the dripping edge
Of the blue clay-stone.

           Now, my friends emerge
Beneath the wide wide Heaven—and view again
The many-steepled tract magnificent
Of hilly fields and meadows, and the sea,
With some fair bark, perhaps, whose sails light up

The slip of smooth clear blue betwixt two Isles
Of purple shadow! Yes! they wander on
In gladness all; but thou, methinks, most glad,
My gentle-hearted Charles! for thou hast pined
And hunger'd after Nature, many a year,
In the great City pent, winning thy way
With sad yet patient soul, through evil and pain
And strange calamity! Ah! slowly sink
Behind the western ridge, thou glorious sun!
Shine in the slant beams of the sinking orb,
Ye purple heath-flowers! richlier burn, ye clouds!
Live in the yellow light, ye distant groves!
And kindle, thou blue ocean! So my Friend
Struck with deep joy may stand, as I have stood,
Silent with swimming sense; yea, gazing round
On the wide landscape, gaze till all doth seem
Less gross than bodily; and of such hues
As veil the Almighty Spirit, when yet he makes
Spirits perceive his presence.

       A delight
Comes sudden on my heart, and I am glad
As I myself were there! Nor in this bower,
This little lime-tree bower, have I not marked
Much that has sooth'd me. Pale beneath the blaze
Hung the transparent foliage; and I watch'd
Some broad and sunny leaf, and loved to see
The shadow of the leaf and stem above
Dappling its sunshine! And that walnut-tree
Was richly ting'd, and a deep radiance lay
Full on the ancient ivy, which usurps
Those fronting elms, and now, with blackest mass

Makes their dark branches gleam a lighter hue
Through the late twilight: and though now the bat
Wheels silent by, and not a swallow twitters,
Yet still the solitary humble bee
Sings in the bean-flower! Henceforth I shall know
That Nature ne'er deserts the wise and pure;
No plot so narrow, be but Nature there,
No waste so vacant, but may well employ
Each faculty of sense, and keep the heart
Awake to Love and Beauty! and sometimes
'Tis well to be bereft of promised good,
That we may lift the soul, and contemplate
With lively joy the joys we cannot share.
My gentle-hearted Charles! when the last rook
Beat its straight path along the dusky air
Homewards, I blest it! deeming, its black wing
(Now a dim speck, now vanishing in light)
Had cross'd the mighty Orb's dilated glory,
While thou stood'st gazing; or, when all was still,
Flew creeking o'er thy head, and had a charm
For thee, my gentle-hearted Charles, to whom
No sound is dissonant which tells of Life.

On Leaving Some Friends
at an Early Hour

John Keats

Give me a golden pen, and let me lean
On heap'd-up flowers, in regions clear, and far;
Bring me a tablet whiter than a star,
Or hand of hymning angel, when 'tis seen
The silver strings of heavenly harp atween:
And let there glide by many a pearly car,
Pink robes, and wavy hair, and diamond jar,
And half-discover'd wings, and glances keen.
The while let music wander round my ears,
And as it reaches each delicious ending,
Let me write down a line of glorious tone,
And full of many wonders of the spheres:
For what a height my spirit is contending!
'Tis not content so soon to be alone.

Fast Friends

The Lover Pleads with His Friend
for Old Friends

William Butler Yeats

Though you are in your shining days,
Voices among the crowd
And new friends busy with your praise,
Be not unkind or proud,
But think about old friends the most:
Time's bitter flood will rise,
Your beauty perish and be lost
For all eyes but these eyes.

The Memory of the Heart

Daniel Webster

If stores of dry and learned lore we gain
We keep them in the memory of the brain;
Names, things, and facts—whate'er we knowledge call,
There is the common ledger for them all;
And images on this cold surface traced
Make slight impressions and are soon effaced.

But we've a page more glowing and more bright
On which our friendship and our love to write;
That these may never from the soul depart,
We trust them to the memory of the heart.
There is no dimming—no effacement here;
Each pulsation keeps the record clear;
Warm golden letters all the tablet fill,
Nor lose their luster till the heart stands still.

Friendship and Love Contrasted

Benjamin Hine

What is friendship? 'tis a name
    Implying love,—not strictly so,—
It is than love a gentler flame,—
    It lights the breast with a milder glow.
We cannot love, but we desire
    To possess the object of our love.
But friendship may the heart inspire,
    If we the object but approve;
And though another should possess
    The object of our friendship pure,
No jealousies rise in the breast;—
    But love, a rival can't endure;
It claims an undivided heart,
    And nothing else can satisfy.
Friendship is content with part,
    And shares with generosity.
My friend may have a thousand friends,
    And I esteem him still the more.
But whom I love, should they admit
    Another love, my love is o'er,—
Or I am wretched; rivalship
    Is the cure, or death of love.
Few have felt the gentler flame,
    And fewer still the last will prove.

Love and Friendship

Emily Brontë

Love is like the wild rose-briar;
    Friendship like the holly-tree.
The holly is dark when the rose-briar blooms,
    But which will bloom most constantly?

The wild rose-briar is sweet in spring,
    Its summer blossoms scent the air;
Yet wait till winter comes again,
    And who will call the wild-briar fair?

Then, scorn the silly rose-wreath now,
    And deck thee with the holly's sheen,
That, when December blights thy brow,
    He still may leave thy garland green.

L'amitié Est L'amour Sans Ailes

George Gordon, Lord Byron

Why should my anxious breast repine,
    Because my youth is fled?
Days of delight may still be mine;
    Affection is not dead.
In tracing back the years of youth,
One firm record, one lasting truth
    Celestial consolation brings;
Bear it, ye breezes, to the seat,
Where first my heart responsive beat,—
    "Friendship is Love without his wings!"

Through few, but deeply chequer'd years,
    What moments have been mine!
Now half obscured by clouds of tears,
    Now bright in rays divine;
Howe'er my future doom be cast,
My soul, enraptured with the past,
    To one idea fondly clings;
Friendship! that thought is all thine own,
Worth worlds of bliss, that thought alone—
    "Friendship is Love without his wings!"

Where yonder yew-trees lightly wave
    Their branches on the gale,
Unheeded heaves a simple grave,
    Which tells the common tale;

Round this unconscious schoolboys stray,
Till the dull knell of childish play
　　　From yonder studious mansion rings;
But here, whene'er my footsteps move,
My silent tears too plainly prove,
　　　"Friendship is Love without his wings!"

Oh, Love! before thy glowing shrine,
　　　My early vows were paid;
My hopes, my dreams, my heart was thine,
　　　But these are now decay'd;
For thine are pinions like the wind,
No trace of thee remains behind,
　　　Except, alas! thy jealous stings.
Away, away! delusive power,
Thou shalt not haunt my coming hour;
　　　Unless, indeed, without thy wings.

Seat of my youth! thy distant spire
　　　Recalls each scene of joy;
My bosom glows with former fire,—
　　　In mind again a boy.
Thy grove of elms, thy verdant hill,
Thy every path delights me still,
　　　Each flower a double fragrance flings;
Again, as once, in converse gay,
Each dear associate seems to say,
　　　"Friendship is Love without his wings!"

My Lycus! wherefore dost thou weep?
　　　Thy falling tears restrain;
Affection for a time may sleep,

But, oh, 'twill wake again.
Think, think, my friend, when next we meet,
Our long-wish'd interview, how sweet!
From this my hope of rapture springs;
While youthful hearts thus fondly swell,
Absence, my friend, can only tell,
"Friendship is Love without his wings!"

In one, and one alone deceiv'd,
Did I my error mourn?
No—from oppressive bonds relicv'd,
I left the wretch to scorn.
I turn'd to those my childhood knew,
With feelings warm, with bosoms true,
Twin'd with my heart's according strings;
And till those vital chords shall break,
For none but these my breast shall wake
Friendship, the power deprived of wings!

Ye few! my soul, my life is yours,
My memory and my hope;
Your worth a lasting love insures,
Unfetter'd in its scope;
From smooth deceit and terror sprung,
With aspect fair and honey'd tongue,
Let Adulation wait on kings;
With joy elate, by snares beset,
We, we, my friends, can ne'er forget,
"Friendship is Love without his wings!"

Fictions and dreams inspire the bard,
Who rolls the epic song;

Friendship and truth be my reward—
    To me no bays belong;
If laurell'd Fame but dwells with lies,
Me the enchantress ever flies,
    Whose heart and not whose fancy sings;
Simple and young, I dare not feign;
Mine be the rude yet heartfelt strain,
    "Friendship is Love without his wings!"

Spring

Sara Teasdale

In Central Park the lovers sit,
    On every hilly path they stroll.
Each thinks his love is infinite,
    And crowns his soul.

But we are cynical and wise,
    We walk a careful foot apart.
You make a little joke that tries
    To hide your heart.

Give over, we have laughed enough;
    Oh dearest and most foolish friend.
Why do you wage a war with love
    To lose your battle in the end?

Friendship

Henry David Thoreau

I think awhile of Love, and while I think,
    Love is to me a world,
    Sole meat and sweetest drink,
    And close connecting link
        'Tween heaven and earth.

I only know it is, not how or why,
    My greatest happiness;
    However hard I try,
    Not if I were to die,
        Can I explain.

I fain would ask my friend how it can be,
    But when the time arrives,
    Then Love is more lovely
    Than anything to me,
        And so I'm dumb.

For if the truth were known, Love cannot speak,
    But only thinks and does;
    Though surely out 'twill leak
    Without the help of Greek,
        Or any tongue.

A man may love the truth and practice it,
    Beauty he may admire,
    And goodness not omit,
    As much as may befit
        To reverence.

But only when these three together meet,
    As they always incline,
    And make one soul the seat,
    And favorite retreat,
        Of loveliness;

When under kindred shape, like loves and hates
    And a kindred nature,
    Proclaim us to be mates,
    Exposed to equal fates
        Eternally;

And each may other help, and service do,
    Drawing Love's bands more tight,
    Service he ne'er shall rue
    While one and one make two,
        And two are one;

In such case only doth man fully prove
    Fully as man can do,
    What power there is in Love
    His inmost soul to move
        Resistlessly.

Two sturdy oaks I mean, which side by side,
    Withstand the winter's storm,
    And spite of wind and tide,
    Grow up the meadow's pride,
        For both are strong

Above they barely touch, but undermined
    Down to their deepest source,
    Admiring you shall find
    Their roots are intertwined
        Insep'rably.

Passion in Friendship

Bernhart Paul Holst

I like to think of friendship as the wine of life,
    The sparkling fluid which ever stimulates the soul;
I like to feel the downy pillow of the heart,
    And breathe the spirit that will deepest grief
        console.
To me it seems the dearest, sweetest fruit of earth.
    Though not complete unless heaven its blessings
        sends;
The fruitage which replaces grief with quickened joy,
    Is found reposing in the bosom of our friends.

I know the stealthy counterfeit in passion's flame
    May melt the heart and later bring remorse and
        grief,
And steal away the virtue which entenders us for aye.
    And cause a falling of the spirit like the autumn
        leaf.
Hence, true love alone in reason must take root.
    And bind with rootlets strong the tender chord
Which anchors friendship firmly at the noontide point.
    And in eternity secures its just reward.

I speak of passion, for in passion there are twain
    When heart meets heart, enthused, as by the living
        lyre,
And here is virtue tested by an inborn flame,
    Proved in the heat of an intense and rival fire;
Though dear, this proven friendship yet is delicate
    And from sheer doubt and cold reserve may
        early die,
But, kept alive by friendly deeds and warmth of soul,
    No earthly hand can break the all-enduring tie.

New friendships, like new wine, are neither strong
        nor pure,
    And ties thus formed may not in trouble stay,
But, ripened by long years and tested by affliction,
    Our friendships will endure through darkest of
        dismay—
Then, let my life with many friends be blесséd,
    And let my spirit rise with the virtue which they
        give.
And let the cordial warmth, the strong defense of love,
    Endure in me and mine as long as I shall live.

You smile upon your friend to-day

A. E. Housman

You smile upon your friend to-day,
    To-day his ills are over;
You hearken to the lover's say,
    And happy is the lover.

'Tis late to hearken, late to smile
    But better late than never:
I shall have lived a little while
    Before I die forever.

Silence

Paul Laurence Dunbar

'Tis better to sit here beside the sea.
    Here on the spray-kissed beach,
In silence, that between such friends as we
    Is full of deepest speech.

A Song of Other Days

Oliver Wendell Holmes

As o'er the glacier's frozen sheet
    Breathes soft the Alpine rose,
So, through life's desert springing sweet
    The flower of friendship grows;
And as, where'er the roses grow,
    Some rain or dew descends,
'Tis nature's law that wine should flow
    To wet the lips of friends.
        Then once again, before we part,
            My empty glass shall ring;
        And he that has the warmest heart
            Shall loudest laugh and sing.

They say we were not born to eat;
    But gray-haired sages think
It means,—Be moderate in your meat,
    And partly live to drink;
For baser tribes the rivers flow
    That know not wine or song;
Man wants but little drink below,
    But wants that little strong.
        Then once again, etc.

If one bright drop is like the gem
    That decks a monarch's crown,

One goblet holds a diadem
    Of rubies melted down!
A fig for Cæsar's blazing brow,
    But, like the Egyptian queen,
Bid each dissolving jewel glow
    My thirsty lips between.
        Then once again, etc.

The Grecian's mound, the Roman's urn,
    Are silent when we call,
Yet still the purple grapes return
    To cluster on the wall;
It was a bright Immortal's head
    They circled with the vine,
And o'er their best and bravest dead
    They poured the dark-red wine.
        Then once again, etc.

Methinks o'er every sparkling glass
    Young Eros waves his wings,
And echoes o'er its dimples pass
    From dead Anacreon's strings;
And, tossing round its beaded brim
    Their locks of floating gold,
With bacchant dance and choral hymn
    Return the nymphs of old.
        Then once again, etc.

A welcome then to joy and mirth,
    From hearts as fresh as ours,
To scatter o'er the dust of earth

Their sweetly mingled flowers;
'Tis Wisdom's self the cup that fills
    In spite of Folly's frown,
And Nature, from her vine-clad hills,
    That rains her life-blood down!
        Then once again, before we part,
            My empty glass shall ring;
        And he that has the warmest heart
            Shall loudest laugh and sing.

A Legacy

John Greenleaf Whittier

Friend of my many years
When the great silence falls, at last, on me,
Let me not leave, to pain and sadden thee,
 A memory of tears,

But pleasant thoughts alone
Of one who was thy friendship's honored guest
And drank the wine of consolation pressed
 From sorrows of thy own.

I leave with thee a sense
Of hands upheld and trials rendered less—
The unselfish joy which is to helpfulness
 Its own great recompense;

The knowledge that from thine,
As from the garments of the Master, stole
Calmness and strength, the virtue which makes whole
 And heals without a sign;

Yea more, the assurance strong
That love, which fails of perfect utterance here,
Lives on to fill the heavenly atmosphere
 With its immortal song.

Unkindnesse

George Herbert

Lord, make me coy and tender to offend:
In friendship, first I think if that agree
    Which I intend
    Unto my friend's intent and end,
I would not use a friend as I use Thee.

If any touch my friend, or his good name,
It is my honour and my love to free
    His blasted fame
    From the least spot or thought of blame:
I could not use a friend as I use Thee.

My friend may spit upon my curious floore:
Would he have gold? I lend it instantly,
    But let the poore,
    And Thou within them, starve at doore.
I cannot use a friend as I use Thee.

When that my friend pretendeth to a place,
I quit my interest, and leave it free:
    But when Thy grace
    Sues for my heart, I Thee displace,
Nor would I use a friend as I use Thee.

Yet can a friend what Thou hast done fulfill?
O write in brass, "My God upon a tree
    His blood did spill,
      Onley to purchase my good-will":
Yet use I not my foes as I use Thee.

Past Friends

We Have Been Friends Together

Caroline Elizabeth Sarah Norton

We have been friends together
    In sunshine and in shade,
Since first beneath the chestnut-tree
    In infancy we played.
But coldness dwells within thy heart,
    A cloud is on thy brow;
We have been friends together,
    Shall a light word part us now?

We have been gay together;
    We have laughed at little jests;
For the fount of hope was gushing
    Warm and joyous in our breasts.
But laughter now hath fled thy lip,
    And sullen glooms thy brow;
We have been gay together,
    Shall a light word part us now?

We have been sad together;
    We have wept with bitter tears
O'er the grass-grown graves where slumbered
    The hopes of early years.
The voices which were silent then
    Would bid thee cheer thy brow;
We have been sad together,
    Shall a light word part us now?

If Thou Hast Lost a Friend

Charles Swain

If thou hast lost a friend,
　　By hard or hasty word,
Go,—call him to thy heart again;
　　Let pride no more be heard.
Remind him of those happy days,
　　Too beautiful to last;
Ask, if a word should cancel years
　　Of truth and friendship past?
Oh! if thou'st lost a friend,
　　By hard or hasty word,
Go,—call him to thy heart again;
　　Let pride no more be heard.

Oh! tell him, from thy thought
　　The light of joy hath fled;
That, in thy sad and silent breast,
　　Thy lonely heart seems dead;
That mount and vale,—each path ye trod,
　　By morn or evening dim,—
Reproach you with their frowning gaze,
　　And ask your soul for him.
Then, if thou'st lost a friend,
　　By hard or hasty word,
Go,—call him to thy heart again;
　　Let pride no more be heard.

When You Go Away

Ella Wheeler Wilcox

When you go away, my friend,
　　When you say your last good-bye,
Then the summer time will end,
　　And the winter will be nigh.

Though the green grass decks the heather,
　　And the birds sing all the day,
There will be no summer weather
　　After you have gone away.

When I look into your eyes,
　　I shall thrill with deepest pain,
Thinking that beneath the skies
　　I may never look again.

You will feel a moment's sorrow,
　　I shall feel a lasting grief;
You forgetting on the morrow,
　　I to mourn with no relief.

When we say the last sad word,
　　And you are no longer near,
And the winds and all the birds
　　Cannot keep the summer here,

Life will lose its full completeness—
    Lose it not for you, but me;
All the beauty and the sweetness
    Each can hold, I shall not see.

The Two Dreams

Christopher Pearse Cranch

I met one in the Land of Sleep
    Who seemed a friend long known and true.
I woke. That friend I could not keep—
    For him I never knew.

Yet there was one in life's young morn
    Loved me, I thought, as I loved him.
Slow from that trance I waked forlorn,
    To find his love grown dim.

He by whose side in dreams I ranged,
    Unknown by name, my friend still seems;
While he I knew so well has changed.
    So both were only dreams.

To a False Friend

Thomas Hood

Our hands have met, but not our hearts;
Our hands will never meet again.
Friends, if we have ever been,
Friends we cannot now remain:
I only know I loved you once,
I only know I loved in vain;
Our hands have met, but not our hearts;
Our hands will never meet again!

Then farewell to heart and hand!
I would our hands had never met:
Even the outward form of love
Must be resign'd with some regret.
Friends, we still might seem to be,
If I my wrong could e'er forget;
Our hands have join'd but not our hearts:
I would our hands had never met!

If anybody's friend be dead

Emily Dickinson

If anybody's friend be dead,
It's sharpest of the theme
The thinking how they walked alive,
At such and such a time.

Their costume, of a Sunday,
Some manner of the hair,—
A prank nobody knew but them,
Lost, in the sepulchre.

How warm they were on such a day:
You almost feel the date,
So short way off it seems; and now,
They're centuries from that.

How pleased they were at what you said;
You try to touch the smile,
And dip your fingers in the frost:
When was it, can you tell,

You asked the company to tea,
Acquaintance, just a few,
And chatted close with this grand thing
That don't remember you?

Past bows and invitations,
Past interview, and vow,
Past what ourselves can estimate,—
That makes the quick of woe!

The Pallid Wreath

Walt Whitman

Somehow I cannot let it go yet, funeral though it is,
Let it remain back there on its nail suspended,
With pink, blue, yellow, all blanch'd, and the white now
    gray and ashy.
One wither'd rose put years ago for thee, dear friend;
But I do not forget thee. Hast thou then faded?
Is the odor exhaled? Are the colors, vitalities, dead?
No, while memories subtly play—the past vivid as ever;
For but last night I woke, and in that spectral ring
    saw thee,
Thy smile, eyes, face, calm, silent, loving as ever:
So let the wreath hang still awhile within my eye-reach,
It is not yet dead to me, nor even pallid.

Strange Meeting

Wilfred Owen

It seemed that out of battle I escaped
Down some profound dull tunnel, long since scooped
Through granites which titanic wars had groined.

Yet also there encumbered sleepers groaned,
Too fast in thought or death to be bestirred.
Then, as I probed them, one sprang up, and stared
With piteous recognition in fixed eyes,
Lifting distressful hands, as if to bless.
And by his smile, I knew that sullen hall,—
By his dead smile I knew we stood in Hell.

With a thousand fears that vision's face was grained;
Yet no blood reached there from the upper ground,
And no guns thumped, or down the flues made moan.
"Strange friend," I said, "here is no cause to mourn."
"None," said that other, "save the undone years,
The hopelessness. Whatever hope is yours,
Was my life also; I went hunting wild
After the wildest beauty in the world,
Which lies not calm in eyes, or braided hair,
But mocks the steady running of the hour,
And if it grieves, grieves richlier than here.
For by my glee might many men have laughed,
And of my weeping something had been left,

Which must die now. I mean the truth untold,
The pity of war, the pity war distilled.
Now men will go content with what we spoiled.
Or, discontent, boil bloody, and be spilled.
They will be swift with swiftness of the tigress.
None will break ranks, though nations trek from progress.
Courage was mine, and I had mystery;
Wisdom was mine, and I had mastery:
To miss the march of this retreating world
Into vain citadels that are not walled.
Then, when much blood had clogged their chariot-wheels,
I would go up and wash them from sweet wells,
Even with truths that lie too deep for taint.
I would have poured my spirit without stint
But not through wounds; not on the cess of war.
Foreheads of men have bled where no wounds were.

"I am the enemy you killed, my friend.
I knew you in this dark: for so you frowned
Yesterday through me as you jabbed and killed.
I parried; but my hands were loath and cold.
Let us sleep now. . . ."

Signature Select Classics

Elegantly Designed Booklets of Poetry and Prose

This book is part of Sterling Publishing's Signature Select Classics chapbook series. Each booklet features distinguished poetry and prose by the world's greatest poets and writers in an elegantly designed and printed chapbook binding. These books are essential reading for lovers of classic literature and collectible editions in their own right. They make perfect keepsakes to own and to share with others.